Home Terra Preta – home-made black soil

What are the reasons for gardening other than a hobby? Bioorganic? There are organic shops if my wages allow it.
Well regardless of the reason here is all about black earth, in the stadiums, application and additional tips related to the soil.

AF176714

The different soils and plants

Plants like most living beings, only want one thing. A place in the sun, a cool drink without ice and food.

The children simply lie down in the sun, while the older ones look for a sun lounger with sun protection. But even in hot countries, children go into the shade at midday in the summer. There are vegetarians and carnivores, such as a Venus trap.

The floors are different too. There are levels from dry to wet. The thistle needs water, but gets by with little, the rice practically stands in the water like reeds. Water lilies swim in it.

Some are very hungry and want a lot of nutrients, others not so much. But how do I know which plant needs what? It is best to "ask" the plant where it comes from.

There are mostly fruits on trees and bushes, most of the forest is on black earth. Fruits are rich in vitamins and nutrients because they give back to their carer what they got.

Vegetables are rarely found in the forests but are no less nutritious, so they need their nutrients too.

When the veggies are the roots, they don't need quite as much nutrition because their food is literally all around them. For example carrots, radishes, potatoes...

Others need more because they have to transport them first and the transport chain has to be well supplied to. Like tomatoes, beans, squash, peas...

Cucumber plants and zucchini also want a place in the sun, but please use sun protection, the leaves cover the fruit due to their size. Pumpkins are the big and small fat ones, the belly doesn't come from fasting. But he also looks out from under the T-shirt, but please don't get sunburnt.

The leafy greens, spinach, arugula, lettuce. Some people, when they are getting served it, say, "this is rabbit food". Well, it's not that wrong. The rabbit comes from the hare. So you can sometimes find those in the meadow without sowing it. Your need for nutrients is average, with too much sun every meadow turns yellow, especially if it hasn't rained for a long time.

BUT there is a difference between a vegetable row and the meadow. If you give a meadow a lot of water, it will be under water, if you give the same amount to a row of vegetables, the water will not be so long lasting.

This is because the roots of a meadow have formed a carpet of roots almost as dense as a felt blanket. However, by chopping weeds, digging and ploughing, we prevent such formation of "weeds" so this has advantages and disadvantages.

Grain is close enough together to form this web quickly. It is a selected part of a meadow.

Another way to recognize the needs of the plant is the larger circle of origin. Tomatoes, for example, come from Latin America, which is tropical.

Therefore, most prefer the plants in the greenhouse, because they like it warm. Potatoes actually too. The winter potatoes are modified, adapted through breeding.

Carrots and radishes, for example, are northern European, so they can be planted quite early.

As a rule, nature does not let you starve. Before the heat or cold season, depending on the global region, there is a peak harvest time when there are plenty of storable vitamin and mineral bombs to survive this very natural recovery period. Then it's poured vigorously so that new deliveries are made quickly and so that we don't have to eat plant fiber leather, there's also a lot to drink during the harvest time, the harvest should be fresh and juicy.

How do I make Black Earth?

A completely natural way that nature shows us as a cycle. An animal or human comes and takes what it needs. The rest stays where they are, falls to the ground and are eaten after all, or rot. The result, residual compost. If things go bad, a hunter comes and the animal or you're on the menu. The skeleton = lime remains.

Then there is a forest and/or meadow fire and coal is there after, which is activated with the next urine. You can also see from the amount of events how much lime and coal is used in relation to the remaining compost. Because harvest residues and leaves are new every year. And we don't set up wildlife cameras to count how often animals go to the toilet in one place. However, we now have all the ingredients. Organic residues, coal and lime. If we also use the toilet with the organic residues, we also activate the coal.

common composter

There is always some lime in the fertilizer, but I recommend determining the final amount of lime only when using it according to the needs of the plants that are supposed to grow there.

As you can see from the picture, mine is slightly raised. I set up a pallet and put a tile on it. This enables the black soil to be removed more easily and cleanly. If you don't know that only organic waste, i.e. no plastic, metal...

belongs in the composter, you have read it by now.

The use of dry toilet

The use of dry toilets is desired without chemicals, i.e. without bacteria killers and the like.

There are 2 methods of separating the dry and wet toilet or draining the entire toilet using shavings or similar organic absorbent materials. If you separate, you can do the dry toilet directly on the compost and with straw or by turning with older compost, you prevent odors and keep the friendship with your neighbors. You deal with the wet part like with the complete toilet - dry it with organic absorbing material.

Construction mixing tank, partially covered by a tile

With the liquid portion or total toilet you can then mix some charcoal or coal and lime.

A small example of coal and lime

Please also seal here with a lid to prevent odor nuisance. Animal litter or mucking out of pets (no litter box), the toilet should be dry. Finally, drying is the reason why we use a litter (shavings, straw...). On top of the compost, however, it can't hurt to add grass, straw or shavings.

maturing time

Normal organic kitchen waste has a lifespan of about 3 years until they are compost **soil**.
Now we also have paper, shavings or straw with us, especially when using the dry toilet or animal litter.
Without the litter, they could use human's toilet directly but surely after a month.
Toilet paper, handkerchiefs... need 1-5 years, but this paper is not a hindrance to plants or seedlings. Some allow seeds to germinate in a folded paper towel. Straw and shavings are not really a hindrance either, in today's gardens mulch is even used as a weed blocker. This means it only takes a little longer, with shavings to germinate and with straw the seedlings only meander through.
However, leaves and shavings lie close together and do not let the air, necessary for rotting, through.
Therefore, you should only add a little to the compost and mix it in well.
Plants are indeed cannibalistic towards other organic residues, so you could also plant and sow between kitchen waste, but the mold and other rotting organisms would not distinguish dead organic material from seedling either. But many fruits and vegitables, on the ground or already covered, begin to germinate when they contain seeds.
Personally, I don't use quick composting agents. Give the floor time too. I'm also wondering how long it takes for these types of drugs to degrade completely.

After 1 year

I once divided it into 3 stages, where I don't classify when which nutrient develops, but more in 3 years. In the first year, fruit, vegetables, processed foods such as salads (cheese are not allowed (in germany) due to the danger of maggots), leftover bread, the dry part of the toilet... have completely turned into black earth.
Litter can also be used after a year. However, it should be noted that litter is used to keep the stable dry and clean.

Spinach in the chip bedding

Here is a not-so-recommended example of bedding with shavings. More frequent watering is necessary. But, not so well received here, fewer foreign plants (weeds).

Straw bedding is less of a problem.

Potato plant in chicken straw

Potatoes are easy by there consume and also thrive in straw, so they have even more in chicken manure straw.

Kohlrabi/kale in drained toilet

For the chip containing direct uses, the germ breakthrough time took 1-2 weeks longer. This doesn't have to be the case with more water, but those who expect it won't be disappointed if the waiting time is a bit longer.

2 Years Composting

So after 2 years, the full composter is only half as full and the grass is mostly gone, the straw is smaller.

Year 3

Do you actually have Terra Preta now? Now I have to correct myself a bit. Terra Preta is not THE black earth if it does not contain enough coal. Most garden compost is therefore not black soil like you can buy in bags. This requires a larger proportion of coal. You also do not have to renew black soil every year.

Does the soil then have no carbohydrates? Yet! But when a tree falls and rots, first you have brown soil/shavings, then soil comes on top. Over time yo have lignite, but much later coal that we then threw into the oven... Slow down with the time, or let forest and field burn down to charring in "lightning speed".

Creation of rows

If you look at the seed packet, there are always 2 dimensions given. The distance between plants and the distance between rows.
Not that nature secretly spreads seeds with a tape measure at night, but we call it the optimum spacing for maximum plant capacity.
That's how we are - we humans.
Of course I won't write this now because nobody can stretch a cord and from this cord in a parallel distance, according to the distance of the seed requirement, can stretch further cords.
"But now i've started this - so!"
First we stretch a cord for the length of the row, preferably a multiple of 4. For the example I now take 4 meters. (or stretch the cord longer than 4 meters depending on the row length and mark the cord at 4 meters with a charcoal pencil, ballpoint pen...)
Then you take a string of 8 meters, on which you make a mark at 5 meters (rest 3 meters).
Take 2 pins and a stick or tomato stick...
Use the pins to attach the end of the string where the 3 meters end. At the zero point of the first cord and the other end at the 4 meter mark. Now take the stick, tomato stick... and walk along the second cord to the 5 or 3 meter mark so that your two cords form a triangle and stick the stick, tomato stick, into the ground.
Using the Pythagorean theorem, you have now staked out a right angle.

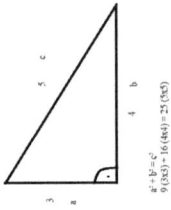

Pythagorean theorem

You now extend the 3 meters over the entire area to be planted.
You can now mark the row spacing on the last lengthened cord (previously 3 meters). Now, if you take a piece of string that is the same row length, length, and another that is the same length as the extended 3 meters string, attach one end to the non-right-angled ends of the triangle and connect the remaining end to form a new right-angled triangle.

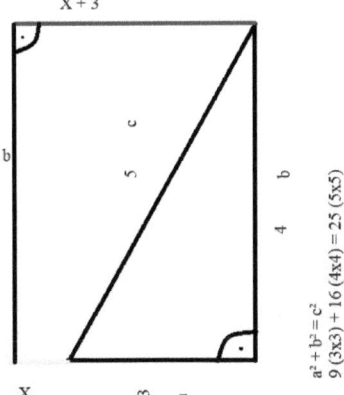

Now you can measure and lay out rows parallel to each other on the 3 +X and on the extended cord - a - rows. So you can measure any surface at a right angle. For example, building foundations and other surfaces.

Surfaces

That's how the Egyptians... measured the buildings. The Egyptians, Maya and other pyramid and temple builders have looked for and calculated a lot by the sun. Or why do many large complex areas from that time have an obelisk in the middle of the square. The sun always rises in the east. And when the architect stands in the square with the rebirth of the sun god, the shadow of the obelisk lies in a line to the west. Now "replace" the shadow with the 4 meter cord or stretch a cord along the shadow.

But since we don't want an obelisk (sun needle) in the middle of the rows of beds, we naturally have to put the sun needle in the zero point and have to extend the shadow to the other side, towards the east. Now we're back to the chapter on creating rows, but we've aligned our rows of vegetables according to the sun.
It is less spectacular but also effective, if you take as line B, a house wall, a straight garden fence or similar straight, fixed reference points.

All year round

In our regions we still have winters where frost and snow have to be expected.
But our botanic trainers have also worked here so that you can not only eat snow globes and pick up ice flowers in winter.
Protected from snow cover in a mini greenhouse or just a foil tent/tunnel you can harvest parsley, for example, just leave a few stalks of each plant. If a trunk then forms, cut off everything above the root. Cress and basil do not hibernate in indoor pots either. Just pick single leaves from a plant at a time.

Parsley and ready-to-harvest winter onions

Or you put winter potatoes and onions under a tunnel or something similar. For example, you can use the rows that you want to use later in the following year when you get the cuttings from the cold frame for such as tomatoes, pumpkins, zucchini and co. So those who love it warm.
So-called grass plants such as Roccula, spinach... can also be sown and harvested several times a year. If you proceed here as with the parsley, you will not have to sow as many new seeds.
Mixed cultures often give their harvest at different times, ensure that the greenery is preserved and keep the groundwater from sinking after rain or watering.
Most of the time the sky gives us water, in the winter it's snow. He gives the plants Water in small sips so they don't have too much water in their bodies, which then turns to ice inside and tears them apart as it expands.
Water grows 9 times its volume when it turns to ice. This would then literally tear the leaves and stems apart.
When the ground is frozen there is no water and the plant goes into total dormancy.

Winter

Water expands 9 times when it freezes. Tear up the plant phases

Raginmund

Plants that only need 1 to 2 months before you can harvest something but don't like the heat that much can then be sown at spring and autumn.
You should also consider whether plants are perennials or just annuals.
What exactly does annual mean?
Annual plants can also come back. The Nature does not look out that plants disappear forever of its own accord. A plant naturally forms new seeds in the flowers or fruits in order to reseed itself.
If you allow this, you only need to remember the location and, with the benevolence of nature, you should also have new annual plants.
If you remove or damage the root of a perennial plant, it cannot come back

the next year. If you always leave one potato in the ground per plant, you will have potatoes there again the following year.
IF vole and Co. dont have plans of their own.

Give to take

Well, we're happy to take – but give oops...
But a pot that is empty must first be filled again.
But what does the earth actually want?
In the past, a 3-field culture was kept. In one year grain and calcium-rich plants such as the tomato and in the following year plants that want more acidity, cucurbits, cucumber plants... then the plant remains were dug up in the fields, vegetable charcoal was mixed in, from time to time and the other organic household waste.
In the third year, the soil was allowed to process and mix the compost ingredients.
Today we tend to go "planless", so we fertilizes the soil completely, no matter what is needed. We don't need to let the ground rest for that. If we would test the PH and lime value, we would save a lot. Unfortunately, there are no longer any PH values on the seed packets. Without seeds and/or left behind roots (carrots, potatoes...) nothing comes.
Well maybe by squirrels, birds... but they don't know your garden planning. Seeds and cuttings are also needed. If you don't grow them in a greenhouse or something similar, you have to reckon with a loss. Some things don't open, are eaten beforehand... Jesus already explained that to his followers.
Another method is that of the native peoples,
I ONLY take what I need, the rest is for the animals (which I can hunt) and for natural self-reseeding. The origin of cultivation was based on a different give and take.
Hunting and gathering was not only unsure in the succes, but also time-consuming. Due to the on-site cultivation, they did not need to search, animals were also attracted that one could be hunted, but above all, they could do other things in the time gained.
Coordinators and shamans could ascend to princes and demigods. Shamans could meditate more and more and and better (what we would call today) trigger quantum physical effects.
Psychic and mental techniques grew. (The bridge to the spirits and worlds of the gods grew among other things.)
Last but not least, I also need water. A lot comes from the rain, from above, but in the summer you have to add it here and there. Because fresh, juicy vegetables are only available with water.

However, too much water dilutes the minerals and vitamins, similar to brewing a teaspoon of ground coffee for a whole pot.
You only have a water bottle made from plant tissue with light trace minerals that just cost you a lot of time and money.

The Sun

There are sun-worshippers and shade-loving plants.
But excess should also be avoided for sun worshipers.
Plants that want it warm, that are only planted after the frost season, usually tolerate a little more sun. As already written, some vegetables themselves are not so fond of the sun and prefer to hide under large plant leaves. They prefer their parasol. You should therefore be careful that the earth is not so much an accumulation (small row of hills), but flatter so that the leaves can do there job.
So it is better to furrow the ground a little and then fill the furrow with the fertile soil. Cucumber vegetables even develop toxins in the blazing sun, they also taste bitter. Pumpkins ripen faster before they've even reached their potential size.
A small contrast is the tomato. Well, she was also stolen from Latin America and naturalized.
There are 3 sun zones as viewed from the sun.
In front of the house, hedges, sheds or the like. The morning sun hits the plant the most. This is ok for plants that can handle it a bit cooler. The sun makes the plant wake up (open up) but it's not that warm yet. In the evening, when it is still warm, they are more in the shade from the residual heat of midday.
Neither in front of nor behind a building, hedge or similar. This is where the sun worshipers come to place. The plants have the sun when they get up until the sun goes to sleep. If you plant the plants on the north side of something you will also have sun all day but not as intense at midday as the sun is in the south.
On the east side, the plants get up a little later, but have the sun all the time when it's warm enough. If you have hens and roosters or even just a rooster for manure, if you want to sleep late put them on the west side, otherwise the rooster will wake you up with the sun, which can happen as early as 3 a.m. in summer. (On the weekend, before bed?)

All-season architecture

Under all-season architecture I have now referred a hybrid greenhouse.
Of course you can also work in the greenhouse in summer, but then you
always have to water it.
The usual greenhouses are not designed in such a way that the roof can be
opened vertically when it rains. One reason for this is that the rain often
occurs together with the wind and could therefore damage the skylight.
The purpose of such an architecture would be that you can do direct sowing
and that it would not be so problematic if summer came a little later or
autumn a little earlier.
It would be suitable from the hobby gardener to the professional gardener.
In contrast to a normal greenhouse, the walls are mobile on 3 sides.
These 3 walls are pushed together on rails and deposited in the solid wall.
The solid wall is so strong that the other walls can be pushed into it. So they
don't get dirty from the weather when they're pushed together and you don't
need a lot of effort to clean them in the fall.

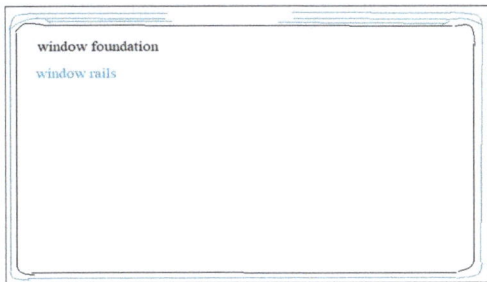

Hybrid greenhouse from above

At the summer time, in order not to damage the rails, a ramp should bridge them in order to reach the rows of plants with a wheelbarrow or similar. The windows are secured to the greenhouse framework with thumbscrew-type fasteners in the autumn to spring and "pressed" onto the greenhouse framework insulation.

The roof is pushed together on top of each other and secured vertically to the solid wall.

The framework of the greenhouse remains unchanged.

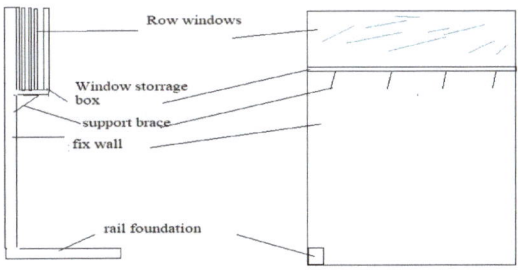

The sprinkler system stays the same all year round.

Regardless of whether you work from the ground with irrigation hoses/channels or from above.

You should not do without the support struts, since skylights have a certain weight, which is often underestimated as a permanent load.

My recommendation every 50 – 75 cm.

The more skylights, the smaller the strut spacing.

So when the walls and roof are pushed together, they have their beds open like outdoor beds.

If you choose a double glass wall for the solid wall, note that the amount of glass walls pushed together is still a strong light block. For sun worshipers you therefore choose the north wall of the hybrid greenhouse for this (fixed) side. For several such hybrid greenhouses, they should take the north side of their planting area. (see The Sun in the previous chapter).

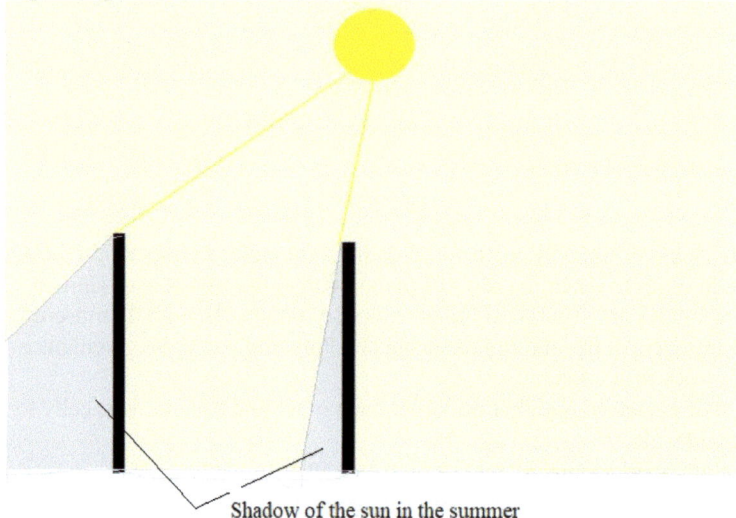

Shadow of the sun in the summer

In the future

The problem we are seeing today, in addition to warming, is falling groundwater levels.
One reason for this is the farmland areas.
Huge areas of agricultural land stand empty during their idle time. This means when it rains there are no roots to hold the water in the ground.
It simply seeps away and immediately drains underground again.

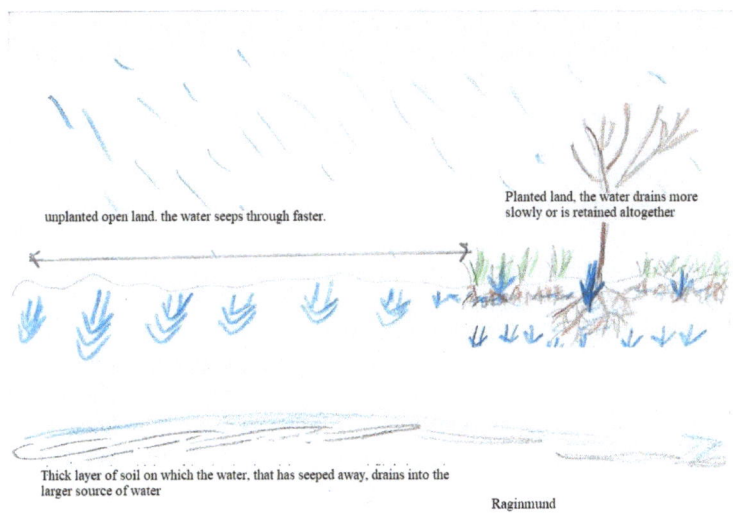

unplanted open land, the water seeps through faster.

Planted land, the water drains more slowly or is retained altogether

Thick layer of soil on which the water, that has seeped away, drains into the larger source of water

Raginmund

Farmland areas in "idle time"

The soil dries out particularly quickly between the harvest and a second cultivation until new roots develop.

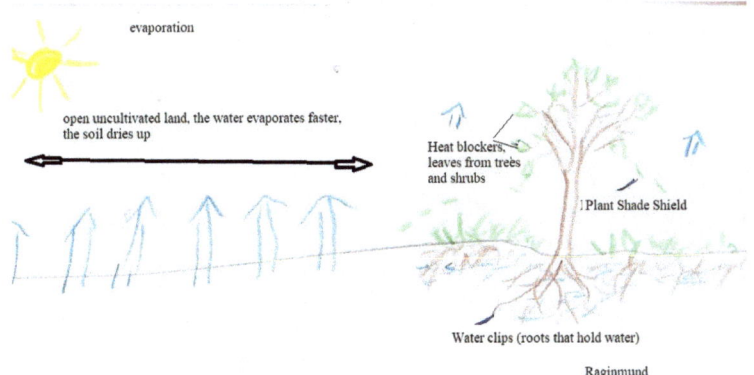

evaporation

open uncultivated land, the water evaporates faster, the soil dries up

Heat blockers, leaves from trees and shrubs

Plant Shade Shield

Water clips (roots that hold water)

Raginmund

Summer inactivity time until new roots form

The problem is that the larger, the open area, the faster the soil dries out. The smaller the area, the more difficult it is to work the soil with heavy machinery.
It is also all the more difficult not to injure the roots of the rows of trees.
If you build tubs in which there is field soil, there would be standing water

in time of heavy rain. One possibility would be to build the tubs with imitation roots. These slow down the water, but when it seeps away, it keeps water in the tissue from evaporating.

However, the mesh must be deeper than the machine soil tillage depth in order not to damage the mesh during soil tillage. It must also be deeper than the expected root depth. So that the roots do not intertwine with the tissue and thus do not close the gaps in the net and the tissue is not damaged during harvest.

But later there will be fewer machines driving in the fields, instead there will be rails along the lengths of the fields and on which a machine bridge driving when it pulls the digger or the plough.

Then hovering robots insert the preferred mixed culture or use it with a grid from the bridge machine. When direct sowing, the grid is then adjusted so that there is space for the second culture, which is sown a little later. The same procedure of stopping the gap, in case of leprosy of the second culture.

The seed cannulas are slightly flexible and equipped with sensors so that they do not accidentally damage the young plants.

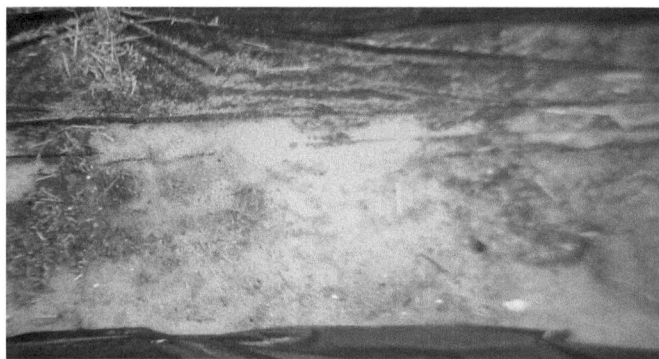

The earth is darker to the right and left, in the middle the seed has not sprouted, water is not held

The harvest is brought in with the same delicate precession. So that in some mixed cultures the gaps are filled with a second sowing.

After the last sowing, grass is sown for winter protection and animal feed.

Planting out a preculture

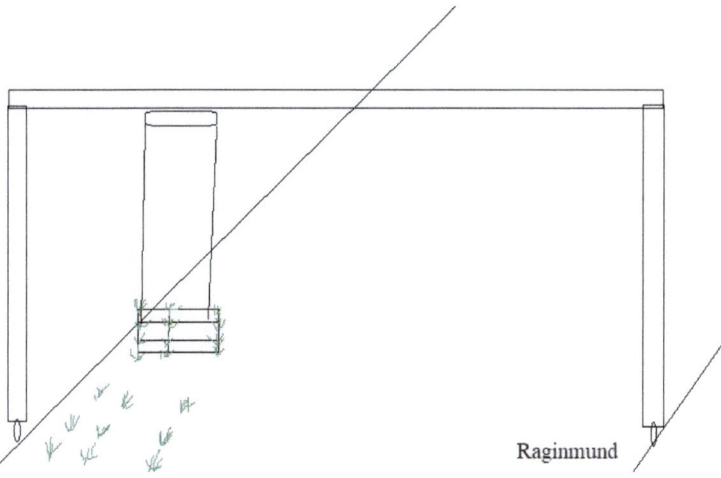

Raginmund

Sunburn protection in the midday sun.
If the plants get too hot then sunlight - insulation screens will come on,
made of transparent tinted solar fan panels or foils. These spread when the
lume and temperature values are exceeded. (lume – light intensity)
In the case of pest infestation, the scents of catch are released in traps and
passed on as bird food... Or appropriate predators are specifically released
and later recaptured again with appropriate scents.

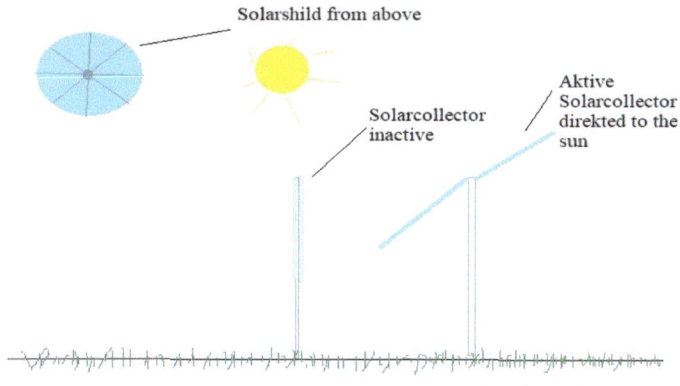

Solarshild from above

Solarcollector
inactive

Aktive
Solarcollector
direkted to the
sun

Raginmund

Drawing solar panels as field plants parasol

The aim here is not primarily to produce electricity, because nobody wants to eat it. But to collect excess sunlight and heat.

Cities will also adapt to survive. Without water and air to breathe, cities will die to health.
In ancient Rome and the Maya, people also had to deal with heat and did not only built on water areas. Their solution was aqueducts and cisterns. These civilizations had the global warming period even without heavy industry. But our industry isn't just polluting, either. So we need air purifiers and why not take some that cover other needs besides clean air. However, we also do not want to have heavily contaminated herbs or fruits on our plates that do us more harm than good.
Sorry Doctor, I'm glad you're there when I need one, but not glad I have to stay sick so you're needed.

Metropoles today

small villages and Cities with gardens

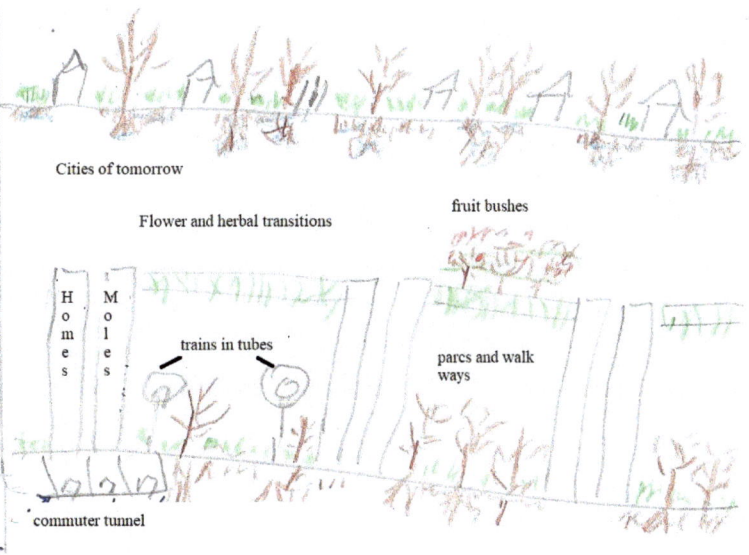

Cities of tomorrow

Flower and herbal transitions

fruit bushes

Homes

Moles

trains in tubes

parcs and walk ways

commuter tunnel

Raginmund

Sources

Unfortunately, I cannot write down all the sources for you, I have been dealing with nature conservation for several decades. Black earth is only a very minor issue. So here are some of the most recent and current sources.

https://youtu.be/V-2IJeFTo9c
https://youtu.be/OMfqNPpkcU4
https://youtu.be/sY0NEmNUzOs
https://youtu.be/jD8n2CKEWtA

Sowing calendar and plant partnership table by „Pflanzen Kölle"
 (German Mole)
https://www.landwirtschaftskammer.de/landwirtschaft/ackerbau/duengung/guelle/verordnung/index.htm
forums and social media.
Like the Native American History Library.
Agricultural expertise from my father from my youth and childhood.

Sources that I can no longer name.
- Why there is still black soil in Africa and Latin America for centuries.
- 3 field culture of the Maya Roman agriculture
- Egyptian Nile Algae Fertilization
- Nature lecture from my training period about the silting up of lakes and rivers

Also, as you can see from my photos, my own experiences.

epilogue

The aim of this small book is to bring you more success in the garden or simply to have explained questions and connections that interested you. The photos are all taken by me in my garden and the drawings are made by me as well.

Articles written by me, some of which you might find interesting, can also be found online at
https://reinesseelenlicht.wordpress.com/delfinschule

For entertaining books from me you will find an overview on the page
https://raginmundart.wordpress.com

For example:
"Dan's Adventures in Africa" (children's book) English/German.
"Broken Code" (Fantasy – Since fiction) German

Manufacturing and Publishing:
BoD - Books on Demand, Norderstedt
ISBN 9783756231966
© Raginmund
all copy right infos by Sabam.be